JAZZ—THE CHICAGO SCENE

THE ART OF
STEPHEN LONGSTREET

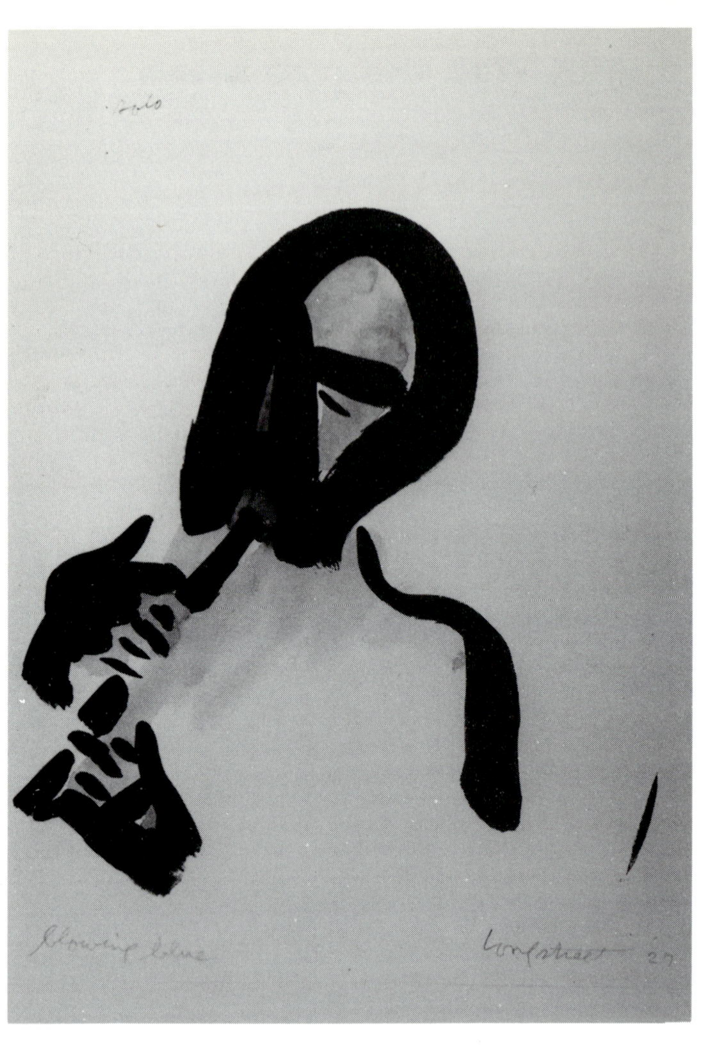

Solo, Blowing Blue, 1927
Ink and watercolor (33.9 x 26)

JAZZ– THE CHICAGO SCENE

AN EXHIBITION OF
THE ART OF
STEPHEN
LONGSTREET

Containing Retrospective Commentary
by the Artist
With an Introduction by Richard Wang

THE
JOSEPH REGENSTEIN
LIBRARY

THE
UNIVERSITY OF
CHICAGO

OCTOBER-NOVEMBER
1989

To be noted: Unless cited otherwise, drawings are courtesy of the artist. In all cases, works of art are on paper, and measurements are in centimeters with height preceding width. Stephen Longstreet used a variety of media in his work, combining them with special effectiveness. Where possible, the various media have been described, including ink, watercolor, lithophoto, collage, felt tip pen, brush, and reed pen.

Printed in the United States of America
Library of Congress Card Number 89-40611

ISBN 0-943056-11-X

Cover illustration: *Dancing at the Dreamland Cafe, 1926*
Ink wash and chalk

Design by Cameron Poulter

INTRODUCTION

Stephen Longstreet's contributions to the history of jazz are well known but none is more alive than his art—his attempts over more than half a century to capture the telling moment, "the real thing." His art, in fact, is inseparable from the story he tells.

We are grateful to Stephen Longstreet for allowing the University Library to combine his art and commentary with historical documentation from the Chicago Jazz Archive. His vibrant, swiftly composed drawings are in stark contrast to the muted images and texts from the archival record. They complement one another in a very special way; the music can almost be heard.

The two parts of the exhibition have been faithfully united by Richard Wang and Kim Coventry. With a sure sense of time and mood, Richard Wang chose the contents of the show, placing them within the Chicago scene. Kim Coventry the Exhibition Coordinator, guided the whole enterprise, including an evocative installation, to completion with tact and imagination. Betsy Bishop was the ever cheerful typist who produced the catalog text on disk, which helped Cameron Poulter design a catalog that captures the artist as well as the spirit of the art.

Robert Rosenthal
Curator of Special Collections
October, 1989

STEPHEN LONGSTREET

As a jazz historian, Longstreet has always been more concerned with, as he has written, "the smell of the real thing" than with any exacting description of the music. He has published five books on jazz, all brilliantly illustrated with his drawings and watercolors. Concerning his first, *The Real Jazz Old and New* (1956), he states, "I didn't write it. I heard it." In it he takes us on a grand tour of the cities of jazz and their joints, clubs, cellars, dives and diverse styles, pausing now and then to quote from his journals, in which he recorded personal conversations with the great and near-great jazzmen.

Of his Chicago years, Longstreet has written, "being young and active I got to know a lot of the natives. Ben Hecht was a dangerous guide and a few others led me to places where I filled my sketch books and did some watercolors of the jazz scene." His intuitive understanding of the originality of Chicago style jazz is a remarkable perception coming from an artist whose only reason for writing books on jazz was to get his drawings in print. His publisher told him they could not publish his drawings without a text—so he wrote books. In respect to Chicago jazz, Longstreet's rejection of the ancient myth that it all "came up the river from New Orleans" is a refreshing perspective. For some time, he has felt that Chicago's role in the development of jazz has not been fully understood; it is his hope that this exhibition will focus attention on the relationship between the city and the music.

Longstreet's interest in jazz has not been limited to the music of the 1920s and 30s; he has continued to listen: "I try to keep up and I always feel one's prejudices should be set in jello, not in concrete." This attitude is reflected in this exhibition of his works. His drawings and watercolors offer an honest portrait of an American art form, one which he says, "seeks a deeper truth or a more mortal atmosphere."

Currently, Stephen Longstreet is assembling his war drawings for a publication to be titled *Pain and Valor*; but more important for the viewers of this exhibition is the prospect of his next illustrated book on Chicago and Kansas City jazz. This exhibition, which coincides with the publication of his most recent book, *Jazz From A to Z: A Graphic Dictionary*, brings Longstreet, as he says, "up to date" in a city that has had a significant influence on his development as an artist and an author.

People know Stephen Longstreet (born 1907) in many different roles, some of which converge, others do not. He has had careers as an artist, novelist, biographer, playwright, screenwriter, journalist, teacher, editor, cartoonist, war correspondent, and, as if that were not enough, a compassionate observer of the human condition. An intimate of William Faulkner, John Huston, F. Scott Fitzgerald, and many of the important artists and literati of 20th century America, he has written more than 100 books, of which at least six have been continuously in print for 40 years. Longstreet attended the School of Fine and Applied Arts of Rutgers University and continued his studies abroad in London, Paris, and Rome. His drawings, paintings, and collages can be seen in major galleries throughout the United States and Europe.

For the present exhibition, fifty-eight of his drawings, watercolors, and collages focusing on Chicago and jazz have been selected from the more than ninety made available by the artist. Longstreet never intended that the captions accompanying his works be published; they came into existence only as reference notes in the journals and sketch books he has kept since 1924. They are written in a style that both illuminates and informs. We are grateful to the artist for the additional captions he wrote especially for this exhibition. (R.W.)

ABOUT THE CHICAGO JAZZ ARCHIVE

The Chicago Jazz Archive is dedicated to the preservation of Chicago jazz. It collects and catalogs a wide range of primary sources, including audio and video recordings, printed and manuscript music, books and periodicals, correspondence, programs, ephemeral materials, memorabilia, and any other germane material that gives substance to the history of jazz as it was created and played in Chicago.

The establishment of the Archive in 1976 was inspired by a visit to the University the year before by Benny Goodman. He had been invited to campus by Mrs. Peter Wolkonsky, Chairman of the Visiting Committee to the Department of Music, to deliver a lecture, "Art of the Jazz Conductor," as part of a year-long series on the Art of the Conductor. The enthusiasm with which the lecture was received prompted Mrs. Wolkonsky and Robert Semple of the Visiting Committee to recommend to the Department of Music that a jazz archive be established at the University. A planning committee was appointed and Professor Richard Wang was invited to serve as the Archive's principle advisor, and subsequently as Chairman of its Executive Committee.

By 1977, Dr. John Steiner, the dean of Chicago jazz historians and preeminent collector in the field, accepted an invitation to join the Visiting Committee and the Executive Committee of the Archive. The first of his regular gifts to the Archive was a unique collection of 3,000 pieces of sheet music relating to Chicago. Many of the historical pieces supporting the present exhibition came from his extensive collection.

The room which houses the Chicago Jazz Archive was made possible by a generous gift from Benny Goodman and the Peter Kiewit Charitable Trust; it was completed in 1982. Mrs. Kiewit is a member of the Archive's Executive Committee and has continued to be a generous supporter.

In 1982, the Jazz Institute of Chicago designated the Chicago Jazz Archive as a repository for its own archive. This body of material includes recordings of the Chicago Jazz Festival and taped interviews of Chicago musicians as part of the Institute's Oral History Program. Two grants from the Institute have allowed the Archive to initiate a limited program of cataloging the archival collections, which is now supported by an endowment fund from an anonymous donor.

Among the important personal collections donated to the Chicago Jazz Archive are those of Bruce Davis, Gordon Goodman, Henry Temple, Robert Peck, Richard Manning, Paul Romaine, and Francis Stanton.

In serving its function as a focus for research within the University, the Chicago Jazz Archive provides sources for the jazz courses offered by the Department of Music. The Archive is also accessible to other scholars by permission of the Music Librarian within the Archive's schedule. As a self-supported resource center, the Archive welcomes donations of material judged relevant to the collection as well as contributions to support staffing, acquisitions, facilities, and equipment.

Professor Richard Wang
Chairman, Executive Committee
Chicago Jazz Archive

CHICAGO JAZZ CLUBS

DANCING AT THE DREAMLAND CAFE

1926

Ink wash and chalk (52.5 x 75.5)

The dancers seemed part of a larger stage set outside in the streets, the city. You didn't know your partner most of the time—just be united by the sound of this kind of music—made just for you and me. Who are all the other guys?

CHICAGO

UNDATED

Crayon and ink (29 x 21.7)

When the Royal Gardens, De Luxe Cafe, and Pony Moore's were in their nights of glory the best jazz was in the air and the crowds were thick as the smoky notes of King Oliver's music and the voices of the blues singers. It was a city, part of it home from a war, dominated by politics hardly honest, and an underworld entering popular literature. All to the sound of a new music.

LAMB'S CAFE

1931

Ink and watercolor (29.6 x 20.3)

There was always somebody noodling the piano at Lamb's Cafe or at the Plantation, and a singer trying out *I'm Crazy Bout My Lovin'* or *I've Got a Feeling*. The early customers liked it lively and as the night grew late it was time to give out the sad blues, the low down sadness of you and the lonely night ahead of you. But there was gin and laughter, new friends and someone to ask "What you playing there?"

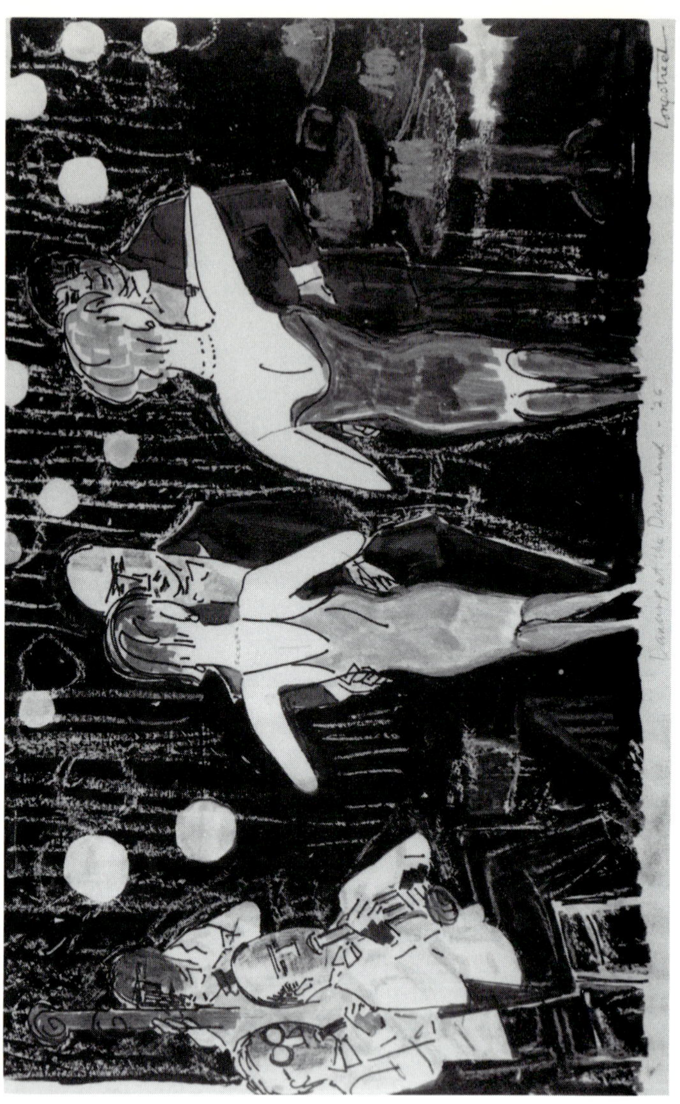

Dancing at the Dreamland Cafe, 1926
Ink wash and chalk (52.5 x 75.5)

CUTTING LOOSE OFF RANDOLPH STREET

1931

Watercolor and ink (27.7 x 21.5)

Off Randolph Street there would be various jazz groups—forming, reforming—taking a gig—trying out new material, telling big stories, and borrowing a buck. All waiting for Lady Luck to tap them. Mostly they played very good jazz, sometimes happy, sometimes sad. Entertainers permitted on the fringe of society. And if black and whites mixed their interests in the music, it had to be in private.

JAZZ MACHINE

1925

Ink and collage (28 x 21.7)

You'd go into Kelly's Stables and the band didn't look so good and the crowd looked edgy. The band—were they on something or full of Capone's rotgut? But once they went into *Everybody Loves My Baby* the sound was coming through right and the round shouldered kid at the upright had opened the sounding board and padded the strings with newspapers. He was riding a sustained pedal and punishing the percussion. When they hit *Suitcase Blues* one knew it was going to be a good Saturday night after all.

ROYAL GARDEN BLUES

1926

Tempera and ink (62.5 x 45.5)

In a blue mist—or shifting mists of tattered color it was like a tropical fish bowl life. The dames all ready, the dudes were Johns or Hoods. Or just Joe Blow on the town for a night.

JAZZ BALL, "DAGO's"

1926

Watercolor on lithophoto print (21.5 x 27.2)

This was an early print—hand colored that turned out to be very popular. During a hard winter there was a little art dealer on South Market Street who would buy two or three copies, and take care of coffee and cakes for a while. The jazz players liked my drawings and watercolors but when I gave the cats copies they soon left them around; lost them or tried to pay the rent with them. No dice.

BODY ACTION

UNDATED

Watercolor and ink (27.9 x 21.5)

In the 1920s, the 1930s—dance contests were the rage from the Chicago Daily News Gold Harvest, to college cutting contests, and the Depression's dance marathons. Dancing was class at the Savoy, posh grace at the Rainbow, staid society for charity at the Parker House, a rent party South of the Loop. From Arthur Murray's step factories to Fred Astaire Dance Studios (in name only) "cutting a rug" was the thing.

FRIAR'S INN

UNDATED

Ink (46 x 38.5)

Friar's Inn would often get a holiday crowd of Easter vacation college boys and flappers and paunchy business sports. The band kind of acts up and tries out chords and take their solos more daring than usual and the band canary "was thinking she was Chippie Hill belting out *Pratt City Blues.*" A rummy at a table said it was like the first time Tom Brown appeared at Lamb's Cafe.

HONKY TONK SINGER

1933

Ink (55.5 x 47)

"If you don't want my peaches stop shaking my tree."

They could be impressive these belters of the salty lyrics, the suggestive gesture. Lincoln Gardens would bring in such a real shouter at times and you'd feel how it had been when the stuff was being born and *Rhythm Crazy* would be followed by *Midnight Stomp*. These old gals in the blue smoke were tough and worn, but a tea cup of gin and a butt of loose packed mufa would send them up for an encore.

POSTER SKETCH

1926

Ink (40 x 21.6)

One of the staff of the Grand Theatre asked me to design a poster for a jazz session a group was giving in a hall during a weekend. I did two sketches, this sketch is one—then I had to go to New York. There were said to be 50 copies done with the silk screen process. I have never been able to find a copy. So much got lost—we never had any idea it would become history one would care to collect. And where would it be kept? The jazz world was as rootless as a breakaway kite.

NIGHT SKETCH

1933

Ink (35.5 x 21.6)

Some of the best Chicago Jazz was played after hours, going from Lamb's and the Elites to jam sessions far into the dawn. Pee Wee Russell, Jack Teagarden, and others in mixed groups trying out ideas, a lot of it in advance of what they played for the customers. Then staggering to their pads to sleep away part of the day. It is to be regretted most of the sessions were never recorded.

DREAMLAND DRUMMER

1932

Watercolor and ink (14.5 x 19.5)

Dreamland often had a drummer that lost his mind among his traps [drums] until he was reminded. Dreamland tried for a funky jazz mood of its own. The place had some special drumbeat sound of its own. *Kaycee on My Mind* sounded different here than in a speakeasy pasta cellar dive among raccoon coats and the Sicilians with their hats on.

"ST. LOUIE WOMAN," GRAND TERRACE, CHICAGO

1936

Watercolor and ink (57 x 27.5)

It was mood, an atmosphere of class, easy romance, also a hint of a crime, the sound of a native music not yet sure it was home. A hint of a river town, a season of floods, the sense of dark secrets to laugh at.

SOUTH SIDE STREET SCENES

NIGHT TOWN, SOUTH SIDE

1925

Felt point and collage (21.5 x 27.7)

It was always a lively scene—barbeque and gin, church music and the reefer man. The street was the show—and so why go home to a cold water flat with the rent man at the door. The heavy stuff-H., horse, mainlining was only for the heavy loaders and you didn't care what your sister did after hours.

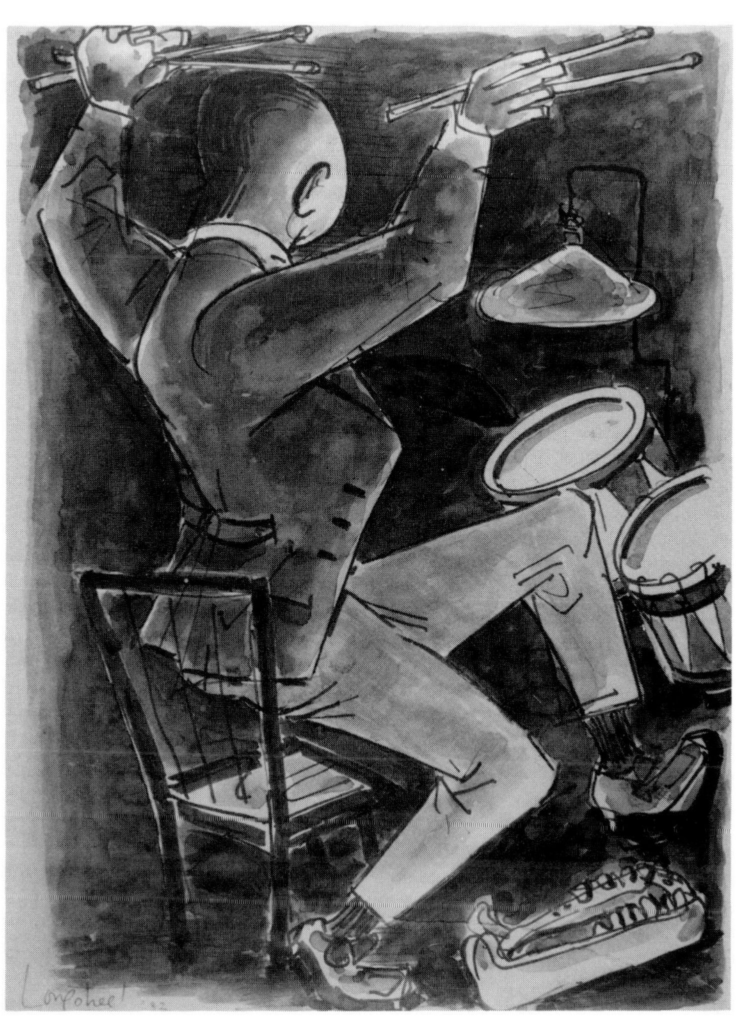

Dreamland Drummer, 1932
Watercolor and ink (14.5 x 19.5)

UNDER THE EL

1930

Crayon and collage (29 x 21.5)

El going south was a crowded world of sellers and buyers of music, dance studios, night clubs, cafes, speakeasies, and garlic scented eating places. There were laughs, tears, and a hunt for a special moment in a drink, sex, music, and then a late El train home.

SOUTH OF THE LOOP

1928

Felt point (27.9 x 21.7)

Chicago Street Scene—busy with music, pickpockets, citizens, and small businesses under the El trains. Living and alive, the sound of radio, recordings, and band run-throughs.

STRIPPING AND STRIPPERS

JAZZ, CHICAGO STRIPPER

UNDATED

Collage (66.8 x 45.8)

Burlesque strippers were often great jazz admirers. But the strippers art ("Who the fuck says we ain't artistes?") can be at its best form to jazz where the drummer is the master of rolls, rim shots, the final *bam* of that final roll of pelvis, hip joints, and rotating navel—with the pudenda sent into space.

BLACK PARIS

1928

Watercolor and ink (28 x 21.5)

"Jazz clubs" were formed to hire strippers. Jazz since the end of World War I excited Europe and many Chicago and New York musicians went over and settled there feeling free of the anti-black pressures at home. Josephine Baker—an exotic jazz dancer—inspired many European jazz folk to become masters of the stripper form. There were many Jazz Clubs without strippers that gave free concerts. American stars toured: Duke Ellington, Louis Armstrong, and others.

STRIPPING TO JAZZ, CHICAGO

1951

Watercolor and ink (35.5 x 21.6)

The bump and grind was as rigid and ritual with tradition as the ballet in *Swan Lake* or the *Nutcracker Suite*. Each artist added just a bit of her own sex drive of space and movement. Betsy used to be famous along the Lake Front. Oldsters remembering her classic grind and bump. *Umbah*, grind and bump—double *umbah*! BUMP! Rumor said she retired to become an Ohio school teacher.

CHICAGO RENT PARTY

RENT PARTY, CHICAGO

1932

Felt point and watercolor (37 x 49.5)

The Rent Party kept the jazz people alive during the depression, very often. Guests dropped coins or a dollar in a bowl and added gifts of booze usually "bathtub" gin. They began cheerfully ended late—or if legs failed—as many as could reach a bed made a pattern of hard times in an indifferent city on a lake.

"BIG AL" AND THE MOB

AL CAPONE ROADHOUSE

1927

Ink (30.5 x 30.5)

Jazz owes a great deal to Al Capone. He controlled a great bit of Chicago's cafes, clubs, and the countryside roadhouses. In need of bands, he had hired many of the jazzmen up from the South looking for gigs. The white boys heard this new music and brought jazz over to the white bands forming and taking on much of the styles of the black ways of playing. Well almost. Al Capone himself liked opera, but the customers wanted Louie, King Oliver, then Benny and Bix.

SISTER ACT

UNDATED

Watercolor and ink (27.8 x 21.5)

The night clubs used a lot of jazz players, singers, and dancers. Capone controlled or owned the clubs and roadhouses and he was the saint of the jazz groups. "The patron saint of the horn man and the hoofer," Toots Harris insisted. The females as singers, dancers, hat checkers, dusky waitresses were called chicks, canaries, broads and dames of course—later the mouse, a dog, a pig, foxes, Judies (from England). Let's skip the obscenities for female's titles.

THE FIGHT

1925

Watercolor and ink (27.7 x 21.5)

"The club world is tough tiddy," Billie Holiday said. Not only the mob, the boozy patron but also the rough trade and the trouble in the menages that made up the jazz world of changing partners and rival ire caused trouble. Duke Ellington's managers would tell his girl singers, "This is a respectful group. Whoever you start sleeping with, starting in this town—that's how you end it, OK?"

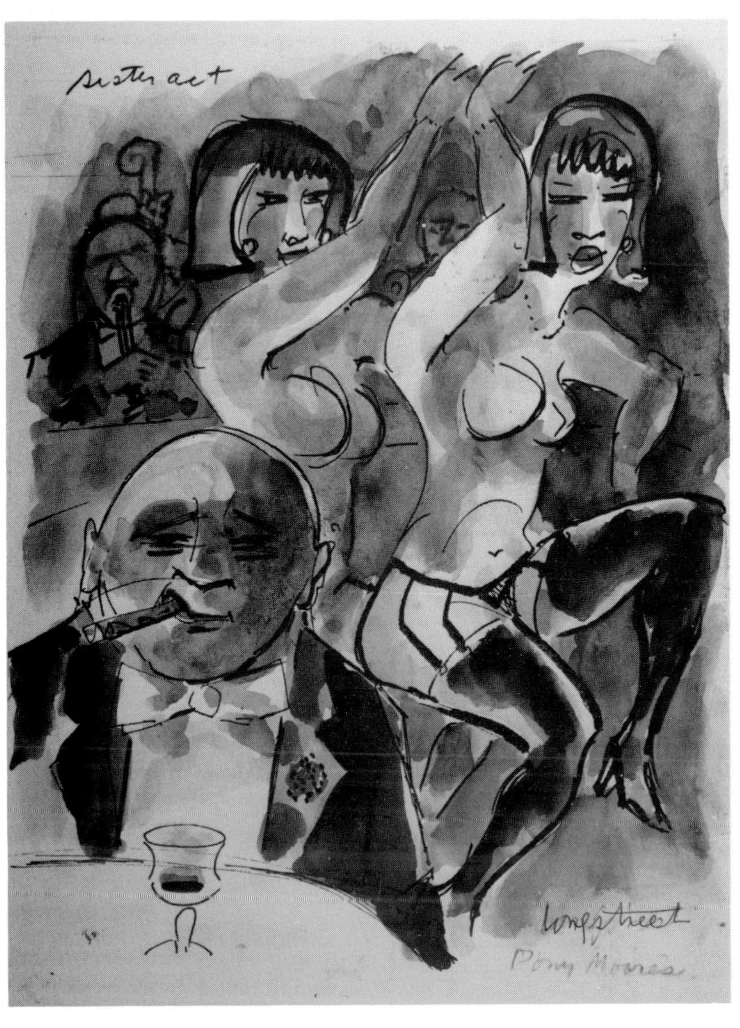

Sister Act, undated
Watercolor and ink (27.8 x 21.5)

LOCAL 208

There are unions and there are places where it's the dirty word. Mostly it's the hall of hope and a greasy deck of cards and you begin to think hope is a dirty word. Then there's a call: a split week at a lake joint, a fill in at a posh club. Dear God a call from Oliver for an alto sax.

UNION HQ, CHICAGO

1933

Ink (45.7 x 37.2)

Sometimes when the mood was just right and the Colombian Gold or Yucatan Red was prime, a trio would get up and improvise around a chord and it was like the invention of the wheel. What came out even the players, mostly, could never do again in just that way and in that combination. It was, to many, the true core of jazz—what you couldn't write down. No arrangement; you had to be there, and open up and let it fly into the night of stale air, human musk, and the magic mystery of sound.

LOOKING FOR A GIG, LOCAL 208

1941

Watercolor (49.4 x 39)

Getting a gig—a job with a band—was the main worry of the jazzmen man or woman singer. There were one night stands as a fill in, a summer season at some crummy seaside, lakeside, mountain hotel or lodge. The jackpot of a national tour. Conventions, radio, even sporting house trio—it was all bread. And you could dream of recordings and some day your own band.

THE PERFORMERS

BESSIE SMITH, EMPTY BED BLUES

1936

Ink and chalk (45.5 x 63.5)

How much of her story is legend is hard to know. Ma Rainey made her—and Bessie finished herself. What is true is her style and sound. That has remained on recordings. She came before the polished singers of the Rainbow Room. Bessie was rough stuff. But precious.

BESSIE SMITH

1936

Ink and watercolor (25.2 x 17)

With Bessie Smith you had to peel the legends and myths away like layers of an onion. Ma Rainey found her. She was in Chicago in 1921 with Sidney Bechet in a show—"How Come." She worked her wonder of style and sound with Armstrong and Henderson. Booze and bad habits slowed her down. She worked private parties, small clubs including those in Chicago—sold gum and candies in theaters. Her death after an auto accident in 1937, and its retelling is still not clear. Was she refused white hospital admittance? Or is the story a black myth?

CHARLIE PARKER "BIRD"

1942

Watercolor and ink (28 x 21.5)

Bird liked to play Chicago if the mood was good in him. Sometimes he didn't show. Often he played it the way he felt it at the moment. The worse time for him I recall was when his daughter died and he broke apart. Even when put together—the cracks, the glue, might not hold. But when the spirit was high the sound was like no other. It was "the Bird" and "the Bird" alone.

(The film "Bird" was a good try—but it was too clever—too much tampering, rerecordings, and only a Faulkner or a Dostoevsky could have written a proper script)

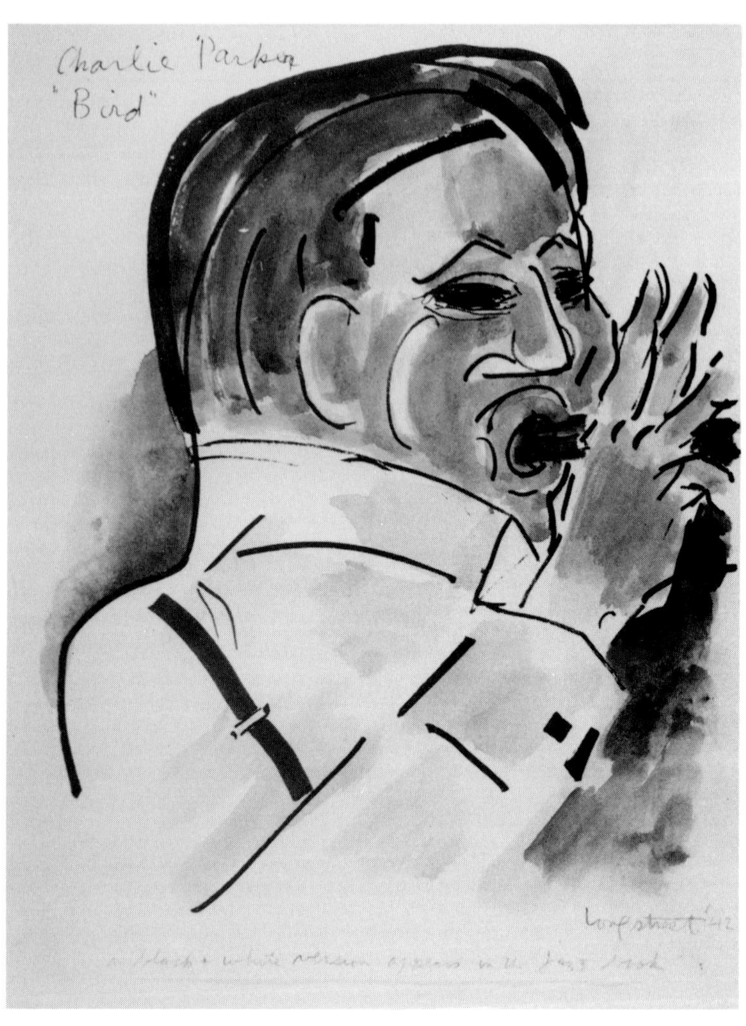

Charlie Parker "Bird", 1942
Watercolor and ink (28 x 21.5)

BUNK JACKSON, 40 YEARS IN JAZZ

UNDATED

Ink (28 x 21.5)

He was one of the best for some time and he lost his teeth and then his lip. He pawned his horn so he was in the shadows a long time. Then someone remembered Old Bunk and got him a set of choppers and a new horn—and he played better than ever. Some stories do have a happy ending. The old jazz motto, "Die young and leave a beautiful body" wasn't always the rule.

SARAH VAUGHAN

1967

Ink (28 x 21.5)

Sarah, a fine artist, drifted between pop tunes and the real jazz (Mancini and Le Grand Shlock!). Her voice is so good and her bop is real amazing with Gillespie, Parker, and Powell. As a vocalist she is among the half-dozen great jazz singers. Ella, Holiday, maybe Bailey. A lot sing jazz. But the real great stuff is rare.

HOAGY CARMICHAEL

Warner Bros. Studio, Between takes of *"To Have and Have Not"*

1944

Ink (28 x 21.5)

You can place Hoagy wherever you want—close to some jazz sound—certainly the man who introduced "Good Jazz" bands into college proms. The composer of music from *Stardust* on to inserts of his talents into motion pictures. Maybe he was a transmission belt between pop and the real thing—and maybe pop—it's been turned in the right direction by those Jazzmen who put some of it into their free wheeling solos.

BASS

1926

Watercolor and ink (28 x 21.5)

Charlie Mingus as an eight year old played trombone, cello, and—in high school took to the bass. He was, by 1947, with Lionel Hampton recording his *Mingus Fingers*. He and Oscar Pettiford were rivals as to who was the greatest bassist of them all. We all missed him when he died in 1979...So many of the old originals were checking out in the 1970s, 1980s. To have so many of them in their last years was good—but sad too—when one has to see "the skull beneath the skin."

TAPS "BOJANGLES" BILL ROBINSON

1936

Ink (28 x 21.5)

The tap dance was at home with jazz nearly from the start. "Jazz and tap dancing," one jazzman insisted, "is like ham and eggs—they belong together." From Bill Robinson to Gregory Hines this has for sure been proved. Bill, and Buck and Bubbles were among Chicago favorites when they appeared here on tour.

HUDDIE LEDBETTER

1949

Collage (97 x 66)

Huddie Ledbetter "Leadbelly" done the week he died. He was more myth than man. But a real folk music original. A lot of what he said, and was said about him—true? Who knows? But his music is real, exists.

JAZZ BANJO

UNDATED

Mixed media (27.9 x 21.6)

The banjo was more than just a field hand's tool. It goes back to the very roots of jazz. And even today it adds something special to a group. Its twang suggests somewhat of the joy and emotions of the black experience in pain and pleasure.

They brought the banjo to Detroit and Chicago up from the South and how they lied and said maybe life was better there than even with the Rednecks and the Crackers.

WITH BENNY GOODMAN

1942

Ink (28 x 21.5)

Special Collections, University of Chicago Library

Benny would look at you from behind those owl glasses and say little. But he was doing things with swing—which became the most popular of jazz forms. The hard cases said, "Oh sure; it's for the squares—easy, sweet, smooth, any mushhead can cut it. It's going to become so God damn sweet."

And it did—and bebop came in.

PIPE

1935

Mixed media (27.8 x 21.5)

The clarinet came early to jazz. It came apart and you could run with it when trouble showed up. It looked complicated, "like a plumber's orgasm" but a kid or a master could make it sing and wail. Chicago saw many clarinet masters: Goodman, Bechet, Dodds, even Coltrane at times. "It was easy to travel with. It came apart and you could carry it in your pocket—never got in the way like a bass."

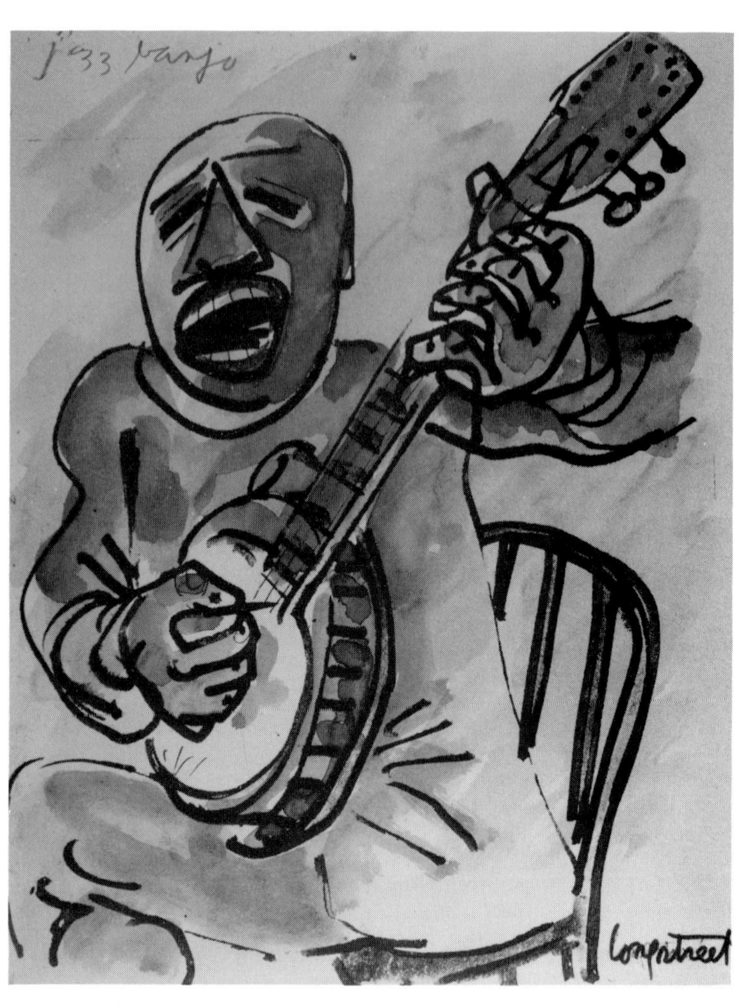

Jazz Banjo, undated
Mixed media (27.9 x 21.6)

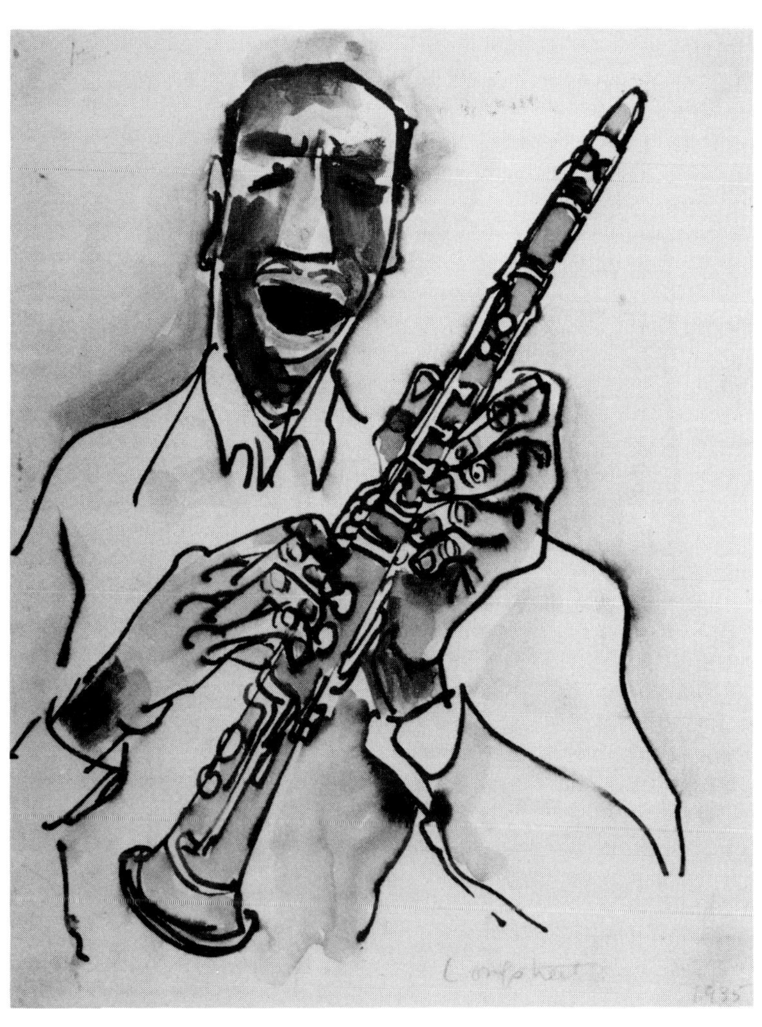

Pipe, 1935
Mixed media (27.8 x 2.5)

BULL BASS

1951

Watercolor and ink (56.5 x 41)

Bass, sometimes called the dog house, its value to jazz was with the drums as a pacesetter. In the back, the last row was mostly where the bass worker did his thing. The man and his instrument were like paired lovers. She, the bass larger, as it should be—didn't the dame nearly always dominate, run the roost?

CHERRY STREET DANCE

1927

Watercolor and ink (27.7 x 21.5)

The bassist had a lot to do with pacing the new ideas in Jazz. Chicago was not merely the old Kansas City, New Orleans styles warmed over, but a laboratory of what jazz was to become pointing toward swing, bebop, and other innovations in the music to be. Among those the town heard was Charlie Mingus, the best of the thumpers and pluckers.

PROGRESSIVE JAZZ

UNDATED

Ink (37.6 x 27.8)

Progressive Jazz—you changed it a little here and there. Chicago heard Kansas City style and New Orleans and made it over. It came to the white boys, Wolverines. Then came swing and bebop and cool jazz and ahead was rock—fusion. Oh hell professor—ain't we *all* progressive? Didn't we all dream of jazz as being as expandable as a tom mule's mouth?

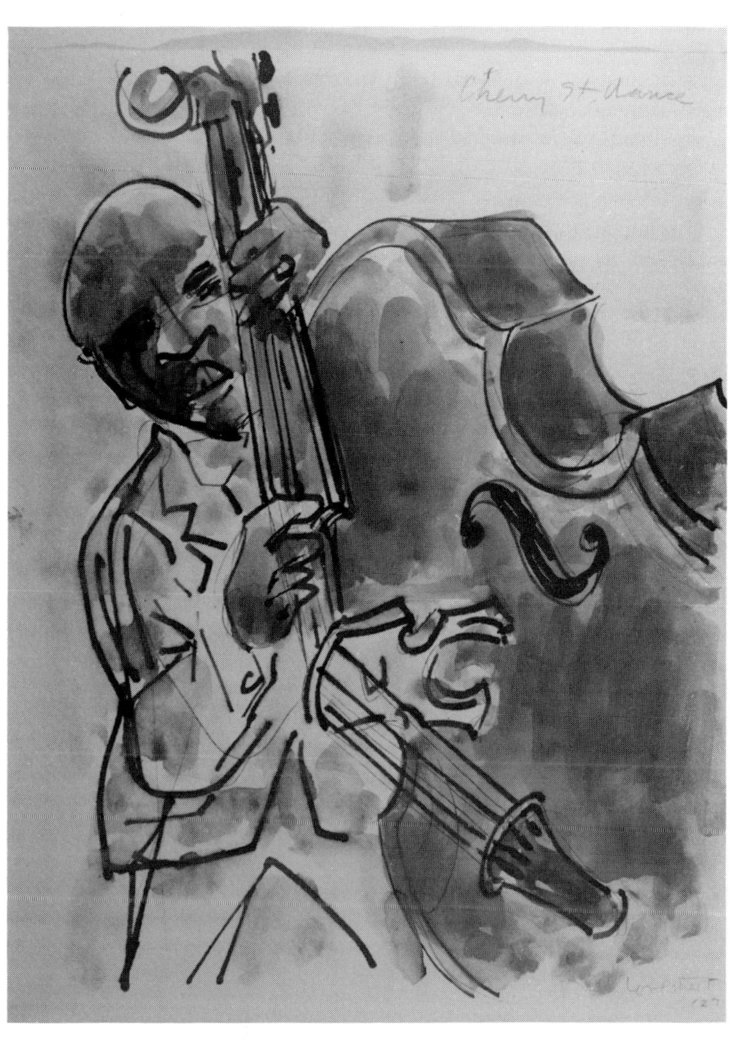

Cherry Street Dance, 1927
Watercolor and ink (27.7 x 21.5)

ELECTRIC PLAYER

1926

Watercolor and ink (44.5 x 28.5)

The guitar came early to jazz, easy to carry up river to Chicago via Kansas City, Memphis, and St. Louis. Even the best of the black guitar pluckers had to give the palm to a Belgian Gypsy, Django Reinhardt. In 1946 he toured here in the USA with Ellington. The guitar had been around, trying to improve on the Gypsy when the electric instrument was being plugged in everywhere. Django remained the best—even if he lacked use of two fingers on the left hand.

LATE SESSION

1927

Watercolor and ink (28 x 21.6)

Chicago white players worked hard to learn from the black jazz and saw not only the merits of this new fine thing but its future. There was no color in Chicago's cultural progress, at least not when it came to music. Pride was in playing Black Jazz. Off stage many black stars had to stay in run down places. It was a good time to get together and try things out, chords and riffs. Night in a boarding house, the beer pitcher being passed round and recalling ancient sessions in long gone places.

PRACTICE

1928

Ink (27.7 x 21.5)

The young at the time grew up with jazz as their only ticket into the tough world. Some could play anything and some damn well. You could begin in a spasm street group and with any luck get a seat in a good band. "It was always laughin' and scratchin' and mooching for a hand-out in them days."

JAZZ FIDDLE

UNDATED

Collage (57 x 55)

Jazz fiddle—the window.
The fiddle was a pioneer folk music tool. The wagon trains west did hoedowns to wild west fiddles. In Jazz too, while not as popular as the saxophone, the fiddle in jazz in the right hand bowing gets respect. Louie insisted, "If in the mood you could make jazz on a hard gal's head."

A MEDLEY OF FOUR THEMES

SOLO, BLOWING BLUE

1927

Ink and watercolor (33.9 x 26)

Chicago gave me a style. As a teenage art student in the mid Twenties I was trying to drop the popular John Held Jr., Russell Patterson styles. But it took time to sluff off the glitz even if it was selling. Living in the jazz world I soon got down to the real hard times, sing the blues, eat the wolf at the door existence of the music makers. I got rid of all details in my drawings—drew directly, no penciling in first—just attack the paper and respect the subject. In time it was original work. Was it good or bad? Who gave a shit when you're inhaling the breath of the real thing.

SING THE BLUES

1925

Watercolor and ink (24.7 x 16.5)

Old voices they never give up. Old Sally claimed to have sung with one of Ma Rainey's touring units. But now she cleaned office buildings, and weekends put on some gamey evening gown and toured the dives singing the *Mandy Lee Blues* and *Oh I love to hear my baby call ma name; She can call it so easy An' dog-gone plain.*

CHICAGO TO HARLEM

1928

Ink (28 x 21.7)

The popular dances get about in the clubs—the true jives. The Charleston and the rest. A lot of them came out of the dance halls of Chicago. Then when they got to Harlem they went into the fast-stepping shows. "Hot Chocolates," "Shuffle Along" and so some even Downtown to B'way. But the road companies came back to Chicago and recast the chorus lines with high-stepping browns and yellows, local dancing talent.

WAITING

UNDATED

Watercolor and ink (28 x 21.5)

Special Collections, University of Chicago Library

You eat up a lot of time waiting for a gig. You talk a lot of tall talk, you study the chicks or the dudes. These are bad habits, the sporting life, and the waiting for good times but you hardly ever throw sevens.

THE COMBO

STRONG SOUND

1949

Lithophoto print (45.7 x 39)

The trumpet player seemed to be the most popular for the customers, their solos the most impressive, and to be compared to Louie or King Oliver was usually enough to call for free drinks. "Bellies to the bar boys!" Horn men were also supposed to be the most horny—even to white chicks. They had a built-in reputation and referred to girls as babes, dolls, chicks, frails, broads, skirts, twists, and sexual images not seen in print in those days.

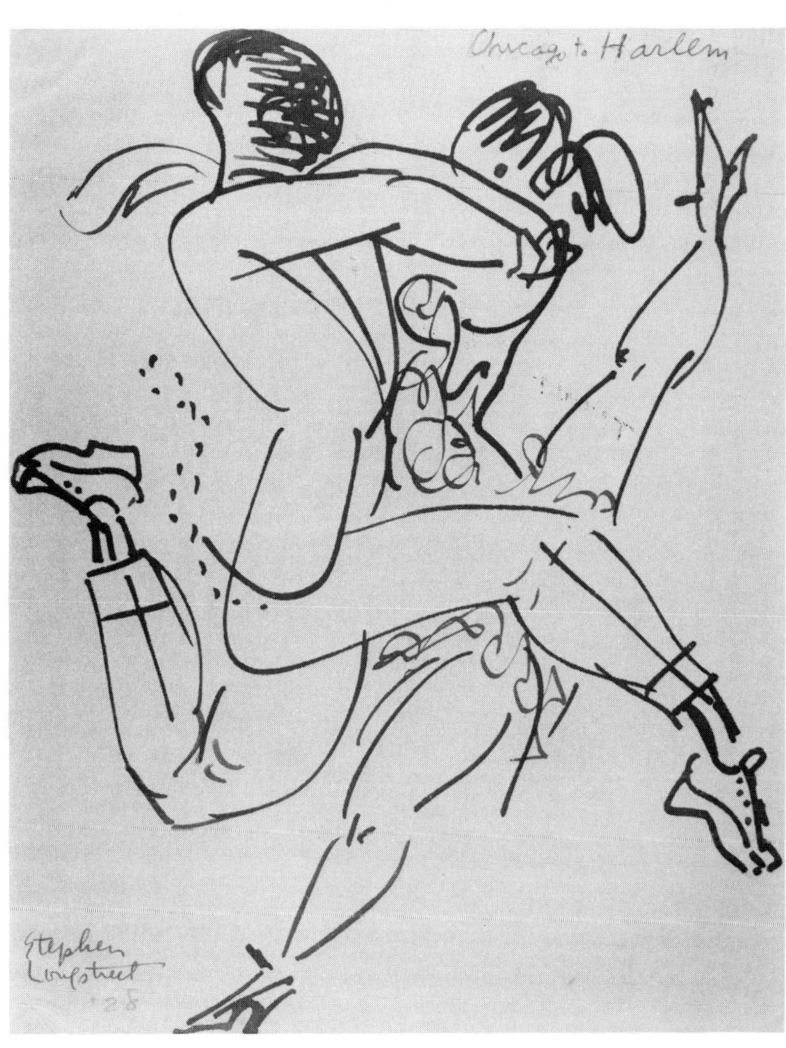

Chicago to Harlem, 1928
Ink (28 x 21.7)

TRIO

1942

Watercolor and ink (55 x 44)

Disciplined jazz resulted when jazz made money in concert. Some group decided to "improve" jazz. Then it was arrangement on arrangement by jazz men who had been touched by Julliard. And critics had written books on jazz as an art form even in French. Much of it often sounded damn good—if you tore up your program notes.

DOIN' TIME

PRISON SONG

1938

Watercolor and ink (49.5 x 41)

The prison songs of Leadbelly are now musical history—but most others produced over two centuries by forgotten men—in agony and physical pain have been lost, this confined music. It did not end with the chain gangs, the turpentine camps, the stone breakers, or the flood control convicts. You can still hear prison songs in an Oklahoma hoosegow, a Chicago jail, the cells of the New York Tombs, the holding cells of Los Angeles' Lincoln Heights cellblock, and the federal slammer of Leavenworth. It's a lament of lost freedom, memories of hungry childhood and open spaces—and sometimes about a two-timing woman.

GEORGIA CHAIN GANG

1933

Watercolor and ink (45.6 x 63.5)

Chain Gang Music: the food was poor, the work mean but the music usually good. Ǵitá, banjo, flute, plenty of these—mostly the blues. The music made real the sound of jailhouse doors, blacksnake whips, the hound dog's mournful bark, and the lone wait for the open gate, and the dime to go home on.

MODERN JAZZ

TIME IS A BEBOP BEAT

1947

Mixed media collage (76 x 56)

Bebop confused a lot of the jazz people. But Parker and Dizzy stuck to it. The beat seemed new and unlike the jazz before; had a lot to do to move jazz forward. Coltrane told some of us— "there is clock time, and now bebop has merged it with Einstein time."

MODERN JAZZ COMBO

1945

Ink (30.4 x 30.4)

Modern Jazz produced such groups as Muhal Richard Abrams, and the Association for the Advancement of Creative Musicians which produced the Art Ensemble of Chicago which produced other avant garde jazz groups that brought in instruments fairly new to the music. The young jazz boys were always pushing the older players—but even an old stud would often sneak a new note into a favorite, or practice a solo "just to see what's to it."

JOINTS AND SPEAKS CELLARS AND DIVES

JAZZ MEN'S JOINT, CHICAGO CAFE

1926

Mixed media (49.5 x 45)

The color lines were still up and night clubs, hotels, eating places cold shouldered black entertainers once off the platform. They had their own Hoofers' Clubs, cafes, and hangouts where the ofays [whites] didn't come but rarely. They were fun, horseplay, hard time hangouts ("Do you have change for a match?"). They could be sad and boozy, also the places of great lies and imaginary Don Juan storytelling. Best of all it had human contact with those of one's own trade.

NIGHT DRINKERS JAZZ CAFE, CHICAGO

1928

Mixed media collage (44.5 x 57)

The cellar joints—speaks, cafes, social pads—were jazzmen and women hangouts after hours. Music better than the hooch.

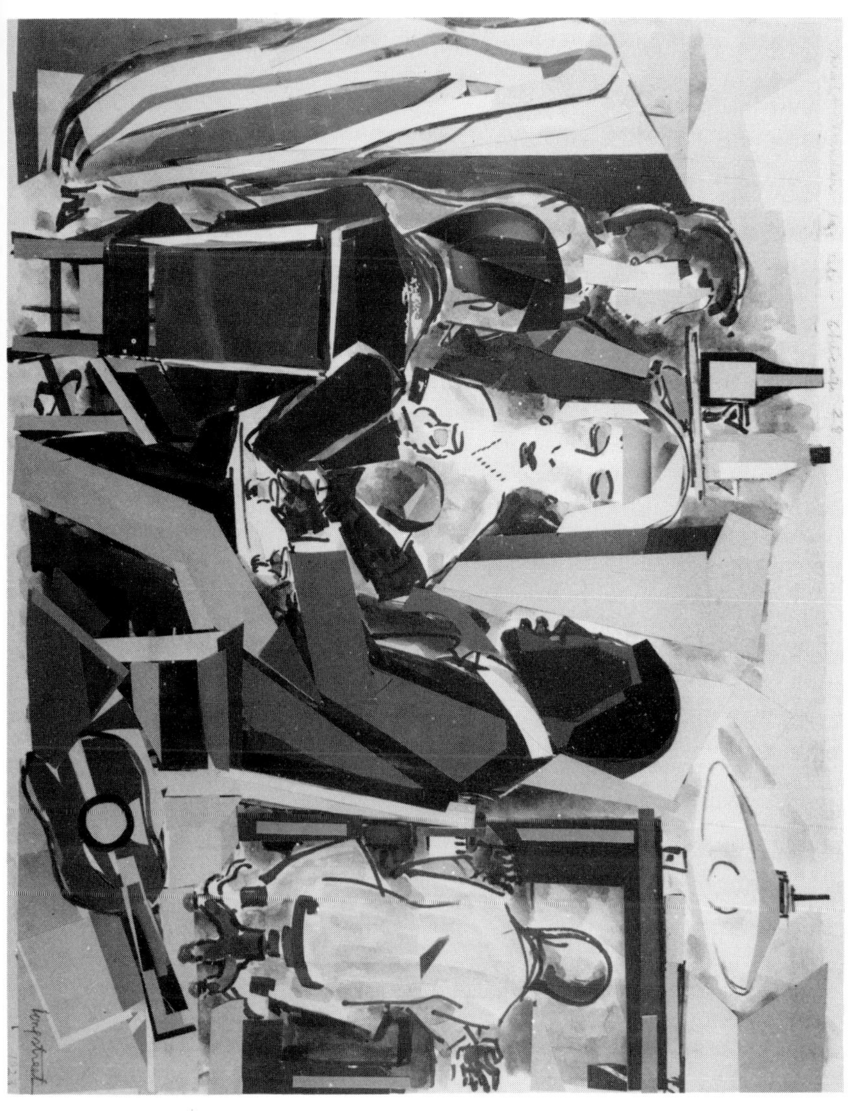

Night Drinkers Jazz Cafe, Chicago, 1928
Mixed media collage (44.5 x 57)